GERMANY

D1046770

Tremsbutter

HAMBURG

Gehrhus
BERLIN

HOLLAND   E. GERMANY

Petershagen
HANOVER   E8

Wilkinghege   E8
Arensburg
MÜNSTER   Hohenfeld
Anholt   Schwalenberg
Lembeck   Achtermann
Engelsburg
Berge
ESSEN   DORTMUND   Trendelburg
Hugenpoet   Sababurg
DÜSSELDORF   Gastätte
Rheydt   Hohenscheid   Herlepsch
Wassenberg   Schnellenberg   KASSEL
COLOGNE   Georghausen   Waldeck   Spangenberg
BONN   Wasserburg
Godesburg   (Hennef-Sieg)   Published in the book *Castle Hotels of Europe*, copyrighted by
Ockenfels   Staufenberg   Robert P. Long, this map is reproduced here through special
Burghaus   permission from Mr. Long.
Alte
KOBLENZ   Klostermühle
Alte Thorschenke   Ehrenburg   Holzberg   Lauenstein
Malberg   Schönburg Waffenschmiede Cleeberg Ronneburg Neustadt   HOF
Zell Reichenstein Sonnenhof Kronberg   Gattendorf
Krone   WIESBADEN   Saaleck   Bettenburg   Banz
Niederwald MAINZ   FRANKFURT   Dürnhof   Thiergarten
Kranichstein   Steinburg   15
WÜRZBURG   Rabenstein
TRIER   Fuchs'sche Mühle
MANNHEIM   Hirschhorn   Neuburg   Weikersheim
Kropsburg   HEIDELBERG Goldener Hirsch Gebsattel NÜRNBERG
Heinsheim Hornberg Stetten   Abenberg
FRANCE   HEILBRONN Lehen Friedrichsruhe   Englburg
Vellberg   Deutsches Haus   Eggersberg
Bauschlott   Falkenfels   Aicha
Badischer   Ort
Windeck   STUTTGART   Furstenec
Solitude   MÜNICH
Sindlingen Weitenburg   AUGSBURG   Seeon
Grünwald
Königsegg   RAVENSBURG   Marquartstein
SWITZERLAND (Bodensee) Wasserburg   AUSTRIA

German Names for German Dogs

By Gertrude Dapper

Edited by
William W. Denlinger and R. Annabel Rathman

Cover design by
Bob Groves

DENLINGER'S Publishers, Ltd.
Box 76, Fairfax, Virginia 22030

Library of Congress Cataloging in Publication Data
Dapper, Gertrude.
   German names for German dogs.
   1. Dogs—Names. 2. Names, German. 3. Dog breeds—Germany. I. Denlinger,
William Watson. II. Rathman, R. Annabel. III. Title.
SF422.3.D36   636.7'001'4   78-52184
ISBN 0-87714-066-9

International Standard Book Number: 0-87714-066-9
Library of Congress Catalog Card Number: 78-52184

Illustrations

The Author, Gertrude Dapper, with one of her German Shorthaired Pointers.

Foreword

Knowledge of the evolutionary history and the early origin of dogs, their primitive ancestor the wolf, or other ancestors in their wild types, is based on discoveries of bone and skull remains from a number of prehistoric forms. Later revelations are preserved in ancient pictographs, wood carvings, copper engravings, and paintings. While a study of the phylogeny of the great dog families is extremely valuable, the primeval origin of our dogs still remains inconclusive. Dogs followed on the heels of man—their tracks lost in antiquity.

It is no small task, if at all possible, to consider the complicated breeding and crossing of the ancient hounds, pointers, and working breeds of Germany. The circuitous routes of the Great Mastiffs, cattle dogs, Spanish Pointers, and Celtic Hounds cannot be analyzed now, although their heritage is still recognized among their descendants. Many modern-day breeds still carry the various shades of black-tan, red-tan (liver) to fawn, a little white on chest and feet, and the black nose. Germany's duty dogs—the Boxers, Shepherds, Doberman Pinschers, Rottweilers, Great Danes, Scenthounds, Giant Schnauzers, and Leonbergers are some of the races having black masks or much black in coat color. This group could also include the Dachshunds and the *Jagdterriers* (Hunt Terriers) but would exclude most Pointers.

Germany can trace an indigenous German Pointer in its earliest known form, with docked tail, at least as far back as the middle of the sixteenth century, for one is depicted in a woodcut by Jost Amman (1539-1591). Later examples were reminiscent of the old Spanish Pointer in color and size. The admixtures of the heavy, red-tan Schweisshund probably fixed the true "roan" color, which is still quite dominant in many of the modern-day shorthaired, wirehaired, longhaired, and rough-coated pointing dogs.

The tractable Shepherd Dog types have also played a part in the development of sporting dogs. It is estimated that other crosses to the old-time shaggy Water Dog (Land Spaniel) have probably produced or at least contributed to the wirehaired and rough-coated varieties through selective breeding.

German breeders have also developed many solid-colored varieties within their breeds. From their native *Wolf-Spitz*, there are solid blacks and browns, and pure whites and wolf grays. The prick ears and the bushy tail, carried over the back, have remained dominant features of the Nordic and Spitz tribes for endless generations.

To the list of the many breeds fostered and perfected in Germany during the last century must be added the smaller Pinschers, Schnauzers, and sport-loving Terriers—many of which are dedicated in their outstanding service for the benefit, welfare, and protection of man.

The alphabetical entries in this book were selected from German pedigrees, the *Jagdgebrauchshund* (1975), and the *Kurzhaar Blatter*. German Stud Books for the Great Dane (*Zuchtbuch Fur Deutsche Doggen*) and for the German Shepherd Dog (*Deutsche Schäferhund*), among others, were loaned to this writer by Sims Pedigree Service. This not only made the task easier but offered a truly comprehensive list of names from a variety of German breeds for comparison and selection.

During this study, it was revealed that some German breeds in this country have become so Americanized by their own individual nomenclature that names of dogs and kennels in most cases do not reflect the country of origin. Perhaps this is better than choosing German-sounding names, selected at random, which may be deceptive in their true meaning. To be sure, a book of this type is long overdue, for today's dogs are worthy of being given names with meaning and distinction.

In addition to the German names in this book, and following the master list, there are specialized lists of English words with the German equivalents (as shown in the *Contents*), which should provide breeders or owners with a wide selection for naming dogs and kennels.

May the German names and words included here be of service to all owners of German dogs.

G.E.D.

Contents

Above and below, Champion
Rottweilers owned by Pamela
Crump Weller, Chesapeake,
Virginia.

Münsterländer or German Setter.

The Name Dog

The name *dog*—where does it come from? In France *Chien* signifies *dog*. Does it evolve from the Hebrew word *Keleb* (or *Cheleb*), which denotes both "lion" and "heart"? Many linguists think it does. It is not known, precisely, just where or when *dog* received his name around the world, yet in the countries listed below, the language symbols and sounds of the name *dog* generate a wide range of communication to serve both animals and mankind:

APACHE	-	GUSE
CHINESE	-	KOU (Peking)
ENGLISH	-	DOG
FRENCH	-	CHIEN
GERMAN	-	HUND
GREEK	-	KYNÓS
HAWAIIAN	-	I'LIO
ITALIAN	-	CANE
JAPANESE	-	INU
LATIN	-	CANIS
RUSSIAN	-	COOAKA
SAMOAN	-	MAILE
SPANISH	-	PERRO
TAHITIAN	-	ULÍ

Above, Great Swiss Mountain Dog.

Above, German Great Spitz.

Above, German Longhaired Pointer.

Below, German Rough-coated Pointer.

Below, German Wolf Spitz.

Dogs of Germanic Origin

The consensus from many sources is that the original ancestors of dogs probably emerged from Asia, the Middle East, and Africa. One of the earliest dogs mentioned, the wild red dog of India, the *dhole*, is described by Kipling as being more fierce than the jackal. The *Dingo* is the only wild animal in Australia that is not marsupial, which tends to indicate it originated somewhere else—probably Asia. Various colors of red, tan-fawn, yellow with black speckling, and also white have been described in connection with these dogs. The gray in various shades, touched with black, is usually associated with wolf-types, similar to the *German Wolf Spitz* and the Keeshond except that the strong tail of the wolf has been replaced by the bushy, curled tail carried over the back.

Still, further speculation lingers regarding the primitive dog types and their relation to modern-day breeds. Contrary to the beliefs of philosophers, zoologists who have studied bone formations of dogs believe "the species are not different, but offer variations which establish points of distinction between types." It is generally known that many original characteristics have been diminished by crosses, mutations, and other factors resulting from adaptations which followed domestication. Therefore, it is presumed that most modern breeds of dogs are man-made, having been developed in various countries under specific standards—not necessarily from the country of ancient origin—to fit the needs of man.

From the early Pariah types, one form has emerged as a pure breed, the shorthaired "barkless" *Basenji* from Central Africa. The Basenji's type in respect to size, color, erect ears, and ring tail has remained true through centuries of breeding. The Chow Chow, or Chinese Spitz, has also emerged as a pure breed from South China Pariah stock which may be traced as far back as the Han Dynasty, for images appearing very much as the Chow Chow does today have been found carved in ancient oriental tombs of that period.

The *Great German Spitz* is said to be a descendant of the *Wolf Spitz*, "native to Westphalia and larger than the other varieties." The *Small*

Above, an early Bloodhound.

Above, Miniature Pinscher. Ch. Jay-Mac's Dream Walking, owned by John R. McNamara, Michigan.

Below, Affenpinscher. Int. Ch. Vinzenz v. Greifensee, owned by Lucille E. Meystedt, Rusk, Texas.

Below, Leonberger Aladin v.d. Zechlesmühle, owned by The Mooring Kennels, Reg., Mrs. Helga Paule, Palgrave, Ontario, Canada.

German Spitz is very similar to the Pomeranian Toy, which was probably bred down in size in Pomerania or in England, where it gained prominence.

Germany has been justly named *The Crossroads of Europe*. From the time of the Crusades, invading armies and merchants found easy access in the west and in the east. Greater fortitude was required of the Roman Legions that crossed the mighty Alps from the south to establish trade routes to Switzerland and Germany and other European areas. They brought with them the Molossus and the Mastiff-type dogs to drive the cattle and to guard them from predators and robbers, or to serve as dogs of war. The influence of the Mastiffs may be seen in the *Great Swiss Mountain Dog*, the *Saint Bernard*, and the *Great Dane*, among others. However, the large and small, the shorthaired and longhaired types with differing structural forms were all referred to as *Sennenhundes* or *Mountain Dogs*.

The Mastiff-type dogs are presumed to be descendants of the ancient Molossus that existed originally in the highlands of Tibet. The old English Mastiff, brought into England by the Normans or the Celts, is most familiar to dog fanciers in modern times. The giant-sized dogs made news in Chinese Chronicles about 1121 B.C., and several centuries later, Marco Polo—called "our original globe trotter"— verified the existence of massive and noble dogs, large as asses. It is not known if the Roman Molossus evolved from the English Mastiff or from Asian dogs.

The *German Mastiff (Deutsche Dogge)*, a descendant of the Mastiff and the Irish Wolfhound, is also called the *Great Dane* in some countries. To the European cynologist, the word "Dogge" still represents a large dog—a powerful dog with more or less foreshortened muzzle, similar to the Dogue de Bordeaux or the Bulldog types with the upturned muzzle.

The *Boxer* resembles the latter variety. German authorities suggest that his ancestors came from Danzig—from the heavy, coarse-boned Bulldog or Bear Dog, and a Bulldog of smaller form, which ultimately traces back to Molossus blood. With tremendous credit going to his German breeders, the Boxer retains all of his early qualities without the ferocious temperament of his ancestors. The Boxer was the first breed selected for police and guard duty.

In subsequent expeditions, other types of dogs came with the Romans and were used mostly to guard cattle. All were required to have great stamina, courage, and fighting ability, which gave rise to the speculation that some of the Drover Dogs that remained behind may have mated with the wolf. Whether fact or fiction, many of these

Great Dane. Ch. Crockerly's Feather, owned by James A. Blood, Sacramento, California.

German Shepherd. Int. Ch. Zoltan Aus Dem Schwarzen Swinger, Sch III, CACIB, owned by Art and Dorothy Levin, Sierra Madre, California.

powerful and trustworthy early dogs were destined, through migration and interbreeding, to foster a variety of new breed types.

The *Rottweiler* is another of the many descendants that claim kinship with the Roman breeds. His ancestors were robust cattle dogs that settled in the Swabian Town of Rottweil, in the south of Germany, for which he is named. Continental authorities believe the Rottweiler carries the blood of the "Roman cattle dogs, the Molossus-like war dogs, the smaller Bullenbeiser (Bullbaiter), and the Alsatian (German Shepherd)."

The large droving and herding dogs of earlier times relinquished their vocation, more or less, when transportation became available. This gave rise to the evolution of Sheepdogs proper, as herding tribes combined their flocks for greater security. Breeders developed lighter and faster dogs—more skillful and alert in protection and guard duties.

The *Alsatian* (German Shepherd) or *Deutscher Schäferhund*, as the breed is called in Germany, is considered to be a descendant of the "old South German Shepherd Dog." Most of Germany's Sheepdogs are thick-coated and white or with fawn shading as in the white *Shepherd Spitz*, the *Pomeranian Sheepdog*, and the shaggy *Poodle Sheepdog*— all of which are highly efficient and are believed to be descended from the same ancestors. During the late eighteenth century, Sheepdogs began appearing at show exhibitions where they were rated for outward appearances which established *type* and pastoral efficiency.

The *Leonberger* is named for the hometown of the breed's creator, who is said to have "crossed a Saint Bernard with a Landseer Newfoundland" and possibly the Pyrenean Mountain Dog. This handsome golden to reddish colored dog with dark mask is thirty inches tall—bitches a minimum of twenty-seven inches. The Leonberger is being bred with renewed popularity, and some imports from Germany are residing in Palgrave, Ontario, Canada.

The *Hovawart* has again become popular for his tracking and watchdog qualities—possibly developed first during the Middle Ages. This is an old breed and was all but lost when German breeders sought to restore its useful type. About twenty-six inches in height, the Hovawart is black or deep golden, similar to the Leonberger as seen in Canada. The farmer's dogs of the Hartz Black Forest region contributed to the recreation of the Hovawart. Official recognition was granted in 1936.

The origin of *Hounds proper* dates back to the earliest centuries of unwritten legend—when first knowledge described the old Celtic Hound as "rough and ugly," with long pendulous ears of multiple folds, and voiced with great tonal quality. As civilization advanced, the Hounds migrated into Europe, from the Mediterranean area, to join the ancestor of all pointing dogs—the Spanish Pointer—to produce countless variations of types of hunting dogs. Their blood is present in most of the Hounds in Europe and England today, as in their other descendants, the Pointers, Retrievers, and Spaniels.

The *German Hound (Deutsche Bracke)* is a combination of many German Hound breeds, and was standardized about 1955. The German Hound is also called the Olpe Hound. The *Hanoverian Schweisshund* was created about 1800 and is said to be a descendant of the Saint Hubert Hound and a lighter type. The Hanoverian Schweisshund has the deer-red coat color of the old German Hound. The *Bavarian Schweisshund* is a lighter version of the old Hanoverian breed—a likely cross with the Bavarian Hound. Many of the old native breeds of the nineteenth century have disappeared in favor of newer types.

The *German Hunt Terrier (Deutscher Jagdterrier)* is a sturdy, rough-coated earth dog, developed by German hunters. This breed was created quite recently from English stock, presumably from a Fox Terrier and the old rough-coated Black and Tan Terrier.

The *Kromforländer* is possibly the newest Terrier breed in Germany, having been developed in the past decade. A rather small dog, about sixteen inches in height, the Kromforländer is white with brown markings on the head and body.

The *Dachshund* or German Badger Dog, which is used in ground hunting and is called *Earth Dog* in Germany, has some characteristics of the Terriers. This old breed, known during the Middle Ages, carries the old Peat Dog blood. The short-legged Hounds appeared through mutations and/or through various crossings and produced the French Bassets and the Dachshund family. Thus, the foundation became fixed for the many low-standing Hounds which have become so important for their type in the modern shorthaired (smooth), wirehaired, and longhaired varieties.

After the year 1848, German sportsmen began developing a number of pointing dogs—shorthaired, wirehaired, longhaired, and rough-coated varieties. Their ideology, to unite all hunting qualities in each type, was accomplished through the formation of breed clubs.

The old native *German Shorthaired Pointer (Deutsch Kurzhaar)* was massive and slow for many centuries as a result of his inheritance from the hunting Hounds, the Spanish Pointer, and the German Schweisshund. The German Shorthaired Pointer's improvement began with crossings to the faster and lighter English Pointers to augment the quality of the Shorthair's nose. Other crosses to the black Prussian Pointers to correct the lack of pigmentation were made under the guidance of Prince zu Solms-Braunfels, from the House of Hanover. Breeders then returned to the old breeds to rejuvenate the land and water retrieving qualities, giving rise to one of Germany's most popular utility dogs—the *Jagdgebrauchshund* or hunting working dog.

The *Weimaraner* is a shorthaired gray or silver-gray sporting dog whose likeness, dating back to the sixteenth century, is painted on a large ceiling in Württemberg. The Weimer Pointer breeders did not begin to develop the modern-day breed until the late eighteenth century. German authorities suggest the gray color may have come from the old native French Hounds in which the color gray occurred, while American records assess the Weimaraner's connection to the old red Schweisshund, an ancestor of the German Shorthaired Pointer.

In Germany, there are also three longhaired breeds—the large, brown *German Longhaired Pointer*, the *Large Münsterländer*, and the *Small Münsterländer*, which are basically white with much ticking, patches, and dark head—resembling the French Spaniel.

The *German Wirehaired Pointer (Deutsch Drahthaar)*, a versatile gundog, was developed by German breeders during the last sixty years by consistent line breeding from the best smooth-coated and rough-coated pointing dogs which were native to Germany.

The *Pointing Griffon* or *Korthals Griffon* owes its existence to E. K. Korthals, who at one time "was associated with the breeding kennels of Prince zu Solms-Braunfels," where he may have conceived the desire to create a rough-coated pointing dog by blending various German, French, and Belgian gundog breeds.

The *German Spaniel (Deutscher Wachtelhund)* has been mentioned by various writers, dating back to the seventeenth century. Regenerated in recent years, this breed's contribution to the longhaired, wirehaired, and rough-coated sporting dogs cannot be measured easily.

The *German Rough-coated Pointer (Deutsch Stichelhaar)* is another very old breed which probably evolved from the German or Dutch Partridge Dog. The rough-coated *Poodle Pointer's* name is an indication of the breed's descent from the staunch Pointer and the rough-coated, game Hunting Poodle.

The *Pinscher* and *Schnauzer* families originated in Germany from various sources. In earlier times, these breeds were referred to as *ratters* or *stable* dogs—having some traits in common with the alert and active Terriers. Their types were proclaimed in the late eighteenth century when the German Pinscher-Schnauzer Klub separated the various sizes,

17

coat textures, and colors under standardized formulas.

The *Affenpinscher*, the little "Monkey Dog," is a very old breed under ten inches tall, whose image appears in a woodcut by Dürer about 1500. It is an ancestor of the Belgian Toy Griffon and several other breeds.

Besides the *Harlequin Pinscher*, under fourteen inches tall, which was established after 1950, there is the popular, smaller *Miniature Pinscher (Rehpinscher)*, which resembles the German Pinscher but does not have the faults often found in dwarf types.

The *Doberman Pinscher* owes the breed name and early development to Louis Dobermann of Apolda, Thuringen, Germany. After Louis Dobermann's death, "his compatriot" *Otto Gäller* shaped the breed through various outcrosses, alleged to have been the English Black and Tan Manchester Terrier and the Black English Greyhound. Uncertainty still prevails as to other crosses. Some German authorities include the Great Dane and the German Hound, whereas American records suggest the old German Shepherd and German Rottweiler, with hunting aptitudes bestowed by the Weimaraner.

The *Standard Schnauzer* is probably the oldest of the three separate Schnauzer breeds, all of which originated in Württemberg and Bavaria, and which also include the *Reisenschnauzer* or *Giant Schnauzer* and the *Miniature Schnauzer*. Here, again, the talented German breeders have displayed the ability to fix three very different types, from various sources, with remarkable results.

German Shorthaired Pointer. Field Born Asta with game taken by her and Max W. Widl.

The Sounds of German

The preparation of this book was undertaken in response to the many requests for a reference manual that would serve as a guide for choosing German names for German dogs and kennels. It is not designed to provide the reader with a calculated summary of the history or the major technical structure of the German language. However, it is necessary to examine some of the essential framework and peculiarities of the language in order to draft a miniature course that would offer an immediate and practical guide to facilitate pronunciation if the purpose for which this book is intended is to be accomplished.

The German language is interesting because of the large number of words that resemble our native English in "vocabulary, idioms, and grammatical structure"—and because the German and English languages belong to the same Anglo-Saxon branch of the Indo-Germanic families which includes Ancient Germany, Germany-Austria, Switzerland, Scandinavia, England, the Netherlands, and Belgium, among others.

The "Romanized" letters are used in this book—the type of letters used in English and widely adopted in Germany and throughout the world. The present alphabet has evolved from ancient times, through writing with pictographs, ideographs, and phonograms. It was the Phoenicians—the travelers and salesmen—who invented nineteen letters of the alphabet, none of which were vowels. The Greeks turned some of the consonant sounds into vowels until there were twenty-four letters in all—basically the same as our alphabet today but not including *c* and *v*. Several changes were then adopted by Latin or Roman linguists to complete the alphabet we use today, the same twenty-six Roman letters.

Since German is a phonetic language, the words and sounds of German are quite easily mastered—if one is to believe that the words are generally "pronounced as they are spelled and spelled as they are pronounced." Each syllable, in German, is pronounced very distinctly and not slurred with another as is often done in English speech. All German vowels are "pure" vowels, which gives one the opportunity to enunciate more vigorously. *No English vowel is the exact equivalent of*

19

a German vowel. The equivalents given in this book are based on English sounds and must be considered as mere approximations.

The building blocks of the German language are the compound nouns and verbs. The combination of simple German words and/or roots or elements of words, become compound or complex words—generally preferred when it is desired to express a complex statement. Under the rules for compound nouns, "Every compound noun takes the gender of its *last* component." And the stress (accent) is generally on the *first* noun. Many new nouns can be formed by adding certain endings to the root of another word, thus making them, strictly, derivatives. One should find no particular difficulty with the very long words because many of the most important compound words may be found already combined in a good dictionary. Otherwise, such words may be located under each component part. A familiar German word, adopted by the English, is *Kindergarten*, which evolves from *kinder*, the plural of *kind* (child) and *garten* (garden). Another is *Burgermeister*, which comes from *Burger* (citizen) and *Meister* (master) Master Citizen or Mayor.

German given names and surnames present few difficulties with declension and with general use. But given names and diminutive names are not always easy to recognize or have no equivalent in English—such

Wirehaired Pointing Griffons. E.K. Korthals, founder of the breed, pictured in 1890 with four of his Griffons.

as *Ännchen* (Annie) and *Florchen* (Flora or Flo, diminutives of Florence). Sometimes the rule about gender is not observed and one may say either *die* or *das Gretchen* (little Margaret). The diminutive given names follow the usual rules—with variants, of course. Familiarity is implied when a diminutive name is used, for a diminutive name expresses fondness for the person or thing mentioned. Diminutive names have a form ending in -*el*, -*chen*, or -*lein*, as illustrated by Gret*el*, Gret*chen*, Hünd*chen* (puppy), or Brüder*lein*. The latter implies *little* or *dear* brother.

Some given names and family names are used for dogs without any apparent dissatisfaction on the part of the beholder, but chosen without any particular acumen on the part of the dog's owner. One commonly finds the German names *Eugen* and *Karl*—but who would wish to call them by their English equivalents? Eugene and Charles? Other names favored are *Ludwig, Franz, Reinhold,* and *Gottfried*, among others. The English versions would be Lewis, Francis, Reginald, and Godfrey or Geoffrey.

In German, *all nouns are capitalized*, as are any other words used as nouns. A proper noun generally remains in the singular when it stands alone. This seems to be true for both masculine and feminine proper nouns. In the *plural form*, proper nouns take -*s* throughout, and this applies to given names as well as to surnames, thus: Friedrich, Friedrich*s*. Some exceptions always tend to apply to rules, and so in German there are masculine proper nouns which end in a hissing sound (*s, sz* or *ss, z, tz, x,* and *sch*) which take the plural *en*: Fritz, Fritz*en*.

In the German language, the declension of articles, nouns, pronouns, and adjectives, and the conjugation of verbs, modulate through a rather complicated framework which varies not only with case but also with gender and number. In these processes, certain words are changed to express various grammatical meanings or relations, causing changes in endings. Most words respond to these declensions under some rather fixed formulas, except for nouns, which are more troublesome.

As in English, there are three genders in German—masculine, feminine, and neuter. The word *the* never changes in English, but the definite article in German, *der* (the), has six forms (*der, die, das, des, dem,* and *den*), depending upon its use in the sentence. With most *masculine nouns, der* is used to denote male human beings, animals, the days of the week, the months, the seasons, stones, and the moon. With most *feminine* nouns, *die* is used to denote female human beings, small animals, insects, and most flowers and trees. It is used with most two-syllable words that end in *e* (die Sonn*e*, the sun). The definite

Left, Longhaired
Dachshund. Ch. Han-Jo's
Victor L, owned by Lee
Bornstein, Minnetonka,
Minnesota.

Below, Miniature Schnauzer. Ch. Pine Needles Playboy Bunny, owned by Owen J.
Clouss, Boise, Idaho.

article *das* is used with most *neuter* nouns to denote countries, towns, metals, and all diminutives ending in -*chen* and -*lein*.

German names for animals do not ordinarily include the articles *der*, *die*, or *das* with a name, but they can be used—for example: Erich *der Jager* (the hunter) or Antje *die Zweite* (the second). The preposition *von* from, by, of) and the contraction *vom* (*von dem* meaning from the) appear to be overwhelmingly preferred in German Stud Books reviewed by this writer. Other prepositions commonly used are *aus* (out, out of) the dam, and *bei* (by, at, near) the sire. One kennel name is *aus dem Schaumburger Walde* (out of, or from the Schaumburger Forest). Other variations are *Bodo vom Tor der Welt* (Bodo from the door of the world) and *Bianka von dem Schönberg* (Bianka from the beautiful mountain).

Kennel names are composed, quite often, to satisfy some traditional magic for breeders, or out of nostalgia for a beloved pet or companion. A name may be a given name, diminutive, or surname, combined with the breeder's locality—a village, city, river, forest, or famous landmark, such as a palace, baronial mansion, monastery, or castle. The term *Burg* was applied to old fortress castles situated at strategic strongholds in Germany, in contrast to *Schloss* which was applied to more elegant castles. Many of these historical treasures have existed for centuries and, in numerous cases, provide a tangible link to the great dog cultural varieties that existed prior to the revolution—with breeding and hunting privileges enjoyed only by the nobility. Today, many feudal castles have been restored and the terms *Burg* and *Schloss* are often interchangeable.

Castle names are recognized for their location, for many are near or within cities. Among the names in Great Dane Stud Books is *Schlossborn*, which means castle born. Breeder Otto Conrady named his Bento, Billo, Brix, and Bara *von Schlossborn*. Also, there are *Burg Dankwarderode*, von *Jägerhof*, *Münchhausen*, *Rommelsburg*, *Teufelsmule* (devil's mill), and the diminutive *Elbschlosschen*—all meaningful to breeders.

Some kennel names appear more euphonious than logical when decoded—except for the inventor. It is easy to imagine the famous names of men and dogs who in earlier times traveled the *Burgenstrasse* or Castle Road from Heidelberg to Nürnberg, or the *Romantische Strasse*, which is only one of the many great Castle Roads where ancient history is all but lost in antiquity.

First names of dogs are usually short, in keeping with registration rules, and they are commonly repeated by nearly all breeders of German dogs in Europe. The breeder's location, name, etc., are only admissible

Left, Boxer. Ch. Random Lane's Hocus Pocus, owned by Dr. and Mrs. Paul Gerard, Sacramento, California.

Right, Doberman Pinscher. Ch. Annheim's Nancy Hanks, owned by Ann Hamilton Mayer, Fair Oaks, California.

as prefixes or suffixes in most German Stud Books. When a kennel name has been granted, it must always be used for registration of dogs by the designated breeder.

German Stud Books and Registration Records are maintained to preserve consanguinity in the breeds: to show proof of ancestry and to guarantee that dogs correspond to the breed Standard. They describe colors and markings (*Farbe* and *Abzeichen*) so exactly that the identity of the dog can be easily proved. The records also include the faults and the virtues of dogs and show whether they have been "Inspected and certified suitable for breeding" (*Angekört*). In many ways, this assists the breeder who is less familiar with faults and virtues of the particular dog.

Some special features of the German language are revealed in the use of nouns and verbs. There are many separable prefixes and a few inseparable prefixes, each of which tends to expand the meaning of the verb to which it is attached. Sometimes the separable prefix to a compound verb is found at the end of the sentence, changing the meaning completely. But the Germanic word order becomes tolerable when one adjusts to finding the verb at the end of the sentence, contrary to English language structure. Inseparable prefixes never leave the word to which they are attached. Some inseparable prefixes are *be, ent, er, ge, ver,* and *ur*—all of which have special meanings and are not accented. The age of *Grossvater* (Grandfather) is extended by using the inseparable prefix *ur*—thus *Grossvater* becomes *Urgrossvater*, meaning Great Grandfather.

The German language does not add the letter *s* to form the plural for common nouns, except for nouns of Continental origin, such as Hotel, Hotel*s*; or Auto, Auto*s*. The definite article *die* is always used for all genders in the plural, but the indefinite article *ein* (a, an) has no plural.

German common nouns form their plurals in one of five different ways. The *masculine* and *neuter* nouns, ending in *el, en, er, chen*, and *lein*, do not change the ending to form the plural. Sometimes the umlaut (¨) is used to modify the pronunciation when placed over the letters *a, o, u,* and *au,* thus: *ä, ö, ü,* and *äü*. The umlaut represents an *e*, now omitted. In some cases the umlaut may be the only indication of plural, as in *Bruder* (Brother)—*Brüder* (Brothers).

Another group of nouns add *e* to the singular to form the plural, as in *Sohn* (Son), which becomes *Söhne*, for it also takes the umlaut. Many nouns ending in *e* form the plural by adding *n, en,* or *er*.

Feminine nouns generally end in *e* and form the plural by adding *n* or *en*. Nouns ending in *heit, shaft, ung, ei,* and *in* are feminine. The word *Freund* is friend (male). *Freundin* is friend (female). To form

25

the plural of the feminine form, the final *n* is doubled and *en* is then added, as explained above. Thus, *Freundinnen* means girl friends.

In many foreign languages, a polite form of address is used. In Germany, the formal second person *Sie* (you) is the polite form whether singular or plural, and it is capitalized. Some words in the German language receive special attention. In compound nouns, when the first noun ends in *e* it is common practice to insert *n* for euphony, or ease in pronunciation. For instance, flower garden is *Blume (n) Garten.*

Accents are not used in the German language as frequently as in the French. The general rule is that the *accent* is usually on the stem syllable as herein illustrated in *Fraúlein*, meaning young lady.

Some German words have final ending sounds where *b, d, g,* are pronounced *p, t, k*–almost voiceless. And the German combination ß, which is used in printed material, represents the double letters *sz*, written *ss* as in gro*ss*.

Since this book was created for the purpose of naming German dogs and kennels, all alphabetical listings, words, phonetic equivalents, and names have been capitalized—although this may not be preferred under other circumstances. Sometimes names are mere appelations of distinction. However, the spelling or pronunciation of German words can easily create an unintentional misnomer. *Heidie* is a very dear German

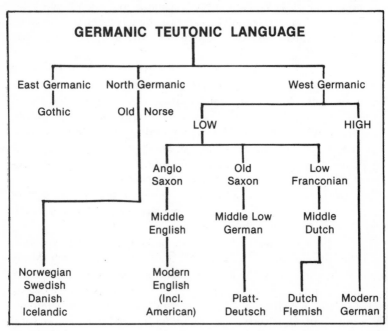

GERMANIC TEUTONIC LANGUAGE

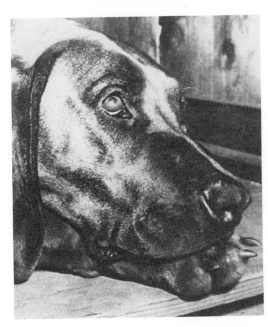

German Schweisshund
(1800).

name, but when spelled *Heide* (with one i) it means heathen or pagan.

German pronunciation is comparatively easy with the following summary of the letters of the alphabet and their phonetic equivalents, substantiated by the *New Cassell's German Dictionary* and compiled with the assistance of German authority and teacher Mrs. Lori Hosking, M.A.

In conclusion, this writer believes it would be helpful to point out that silent letters do not appear in German words, except for *e* in the combination *ie*, and *h*, which is silent after a vowel. German vowels have a *long* and a *short* sound. A vowel is long when followed by a single consonant, when doubled, or when followed by *h*. A vowel is short when followed by more than one consonant, or when *e* is the final letter.

German consonants are pronounced the same as the corresponding English consonants except for the umlauted letters. The diaeresis (¨) is the only aspirate mark used in this book. The letters which differ from the English have been given special attention in the guide below:

Vowels	Approximate English Sounds
a; aa	*ah* as in f*a*ther
a	*a* as in wh*a*t, up
e	*a* as in *a*te
e	*e* as in g*e*t
i	*ee* as in mach*i*ne
i	*i* as in w*i*n
o	*oh* as in *o*ffer
o	*o* as in *o*bey
u	*oo* as in p*oo*l
u	*u* as in p*u*t

Vowels Umlaut	Approximate English Sounds
ä; ae	*e* as in *ai*r, bear (b*a*yr)
ä	*e* as in b*e*t
ö; oe	*eu* as in French f*eu* (no exact English equivalent)
ö	*ou* as in t*ou*r (no exact English equivalent)
ü; ue	*ee* as in s*ee* (round lips as if to say *O* but say *ee*)

Diphthongs	Approximate English Sounds
au	*ou* as in h*ou*se (strong)
äu; eu	*oi* as in *oi*l
ai; ei	*i* as in f*i*le
ie	*ee* as in s*ee*

German Shorthaired Pointer. Fieldborn Asta with deer taken by her and Max W. Widl.

Deutsche Jagdterrier.

Consonants	Approximate English Sounds
c; ts	*k* as in Café, elsewhere as *ts*
ch	*h* as in *H*ubert, strong *h*
chs	*ks* as in wa*x*
j	*y* as in *y*oung
l	*l* as in *l*ip
ng	*ng* as in si*ng*er, not as *ng* in fi*ng*er
q; qu	*kw* as in *q*uote
r˙	*r* as in *r*ose, (*r* is trilled)
s	*z* as in *z*ero
ss; sz	*s* as in gla*ss*
sch	*sh* as in *sh*all
sp	*shp* (at beginning of word)
st	*sht* (at beginning of word)
th	*t* as in *t*op (h is silent)
ts	*ts* as in *ts*e-*ts*e fly
v	*f* as in *f*ather
w	*v* as in *v*ery
z	*ts* as in ca*ts*

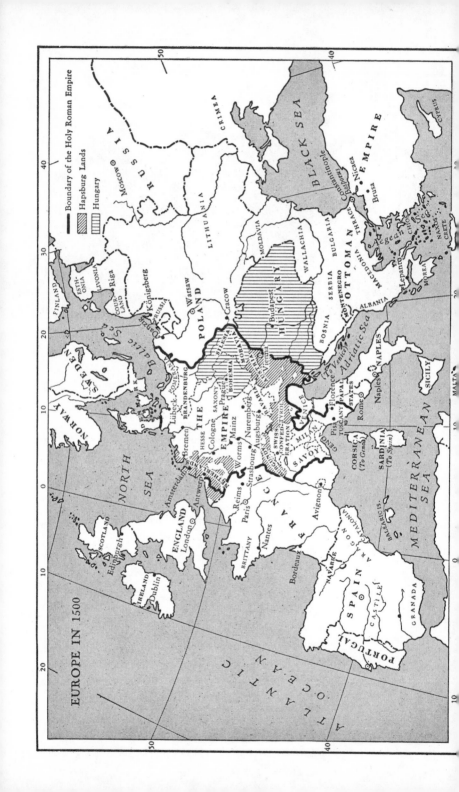

EUROPE IN 1500

Boundary of the Holy Roman Empire
Hapsburg Lands
Hungary

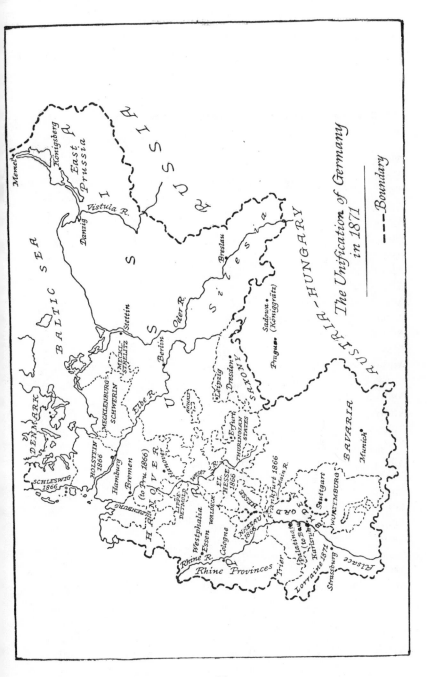

The Unification of Germany in 1871

——— Boundary

31

Alphabetical Listing—Feminine Names

Abbe
Adda
Adel
Adore
Adria
Afra
Aggi
Alexa
Alfa
Alfi
Alma
Amber
Amie
Amsel
Amsi
Andora
Andra
Angela
Anita
Anja
Anka
Ännchen
Annett
Anni
Antje
Areta
Arta
Aspe
Asra
Asta
Astrid
Aurele

Babetta
Bärbel
Baroness
Beata
Bella
Berta
Bessi
Betti
Bettina
Beya
Bianka
Bibi
Bidu
Biene
Billa
Bimi
Birke
Blanka
Bonne
Braulla
Bridget
Briggita
Brilla
Brise
Britta
Brunhilde
Burga

Cara
Carin
Carla
Carmen
Cassy

Carrie
Catje
Catrin
Cecily
Celia
Centa
Christa
Christel
Cilly
Citta
Claudia
Clio
Collette
Comtesse
Connie
Copper
Cora
Countess
Cyra

Daisy
Daite
Dea
Debby
Deine
Dena
Diana
Dinah
Dirke
Dirndl
Distel
Dita
Ditta

Dixie
Dolly
Domina
Donna
Dora
Doris
Dottie
Draga
Drossel
Duchess
Dulcie

Edda
Edelgarde
Eiche
Elba
Elfi
Elke
Ella
Ellen
Elsa
Enrika
Erika
Eris
Erle
Erna
Erra
Esche
Espe
Esta
Etta
Eule
Eva

Fanni
Farrah
Fatme
Fauna
Fee
Festa
Finne
Fita
Flamme
Fleeta
Flicka
Flora
Folly
Frau (lein)
Freda
Frenna
Freya
Frigga

Gaea
Gara
Gerda
Gerri
Geselle
Gilda
Gina
Ginger
Gitana
Gitta
Gypsy

Halle
Hedy
Heidie
Heike

Heldin
Helga
Hella
Helma
Herta
Hertha
Hesta
Hester
Hexe
Hilde (garde)
Holle
Hulda
Hussa

Ilka
Illia
Ilona
Ina
Indra
Inga
Inka
Iris
Irma

Janett
Janka
Jascha
Jenta
Jessie
Jette
Jill
Jlka

33

Johanna	Luise	Onna
Jolle	Lydia	Opal
Juli	Lyra	Oralie
Junne		Orla
Jutta	Mädchen	Orva
	Marga	Osta
Kalla	Maria	
Karin	Marta	Pamela
Karla	Matena	Parma
Kascha	Maya	Patsy
Kate (y)	Mia	Paula
Käthe	Milly	Peggy
Katja	Minka	Perle
Katrin (a)	Mira	Pia
Kimme	Molly	Pierette
Kirsten	Mona	Pille
Kitty	Myra	Pixe
Kleine		Polly
Kora	Nadine	Princess
Koralle	Nadja	
Kyra	Nancy	
	Nanette	Quanda
	Naomi	Quarra
	Neva	Quecke
Lady	Nicole	Queen
Lana	Nina	Quelle
Leah	Nixe	Quenda
Lena	Nola	Querida
Leta	Nora	Quilla
Liebchen	Norma	Quintesse
Liesel		
Lipse	Odessa	Rachel
Liza	Olga	Ramona
Lola	Ollie	Raya
Lorelei	Ondra	Rebecca
Lottie	Oneva	Regina

Rena
Rhoda
Ria
Riga
Rita
Rona
Rosa
Ruby
Ruska
Russa
Ruth

Sabine
Sadie
Sally
Sandra
Sascha
Saxe
Schatzi
Schoene
Sheba
Sibyl
Sippe
Sirene
Sissy
Sonja
Stella
Sus-ie (chen)
Suska

Tanya
Tascha
Tessa
Teufel

Thea
Thyra
Tilly
Tosca
Treble
Tricia
Trina
Trixie
Trudy
Tulla

Ulda
Ulisse
Ulla
Ulrica
Undine
Urna
Ursa
Ursula
Ute

Valeska
Valkyrie
Vera
Verna
Vesta
Vicki
Viktoria
Vilja
Viola
Vroni

Wanda
Wella
Wendi
Wendora
Werra
Wiesel
Wilma
Winnie
Witte

Xandra
Xanta
Xantippe
Xella
Xenia
Xilla (i)

Yolanthe
Yolo
Yunga
Yvonne

Zandra
Zeke
Zella
Zenda
Zenta
Zenzi
Zola
Zolly
Zomara
Zorra

Alphabetical Listing—Masculine Names

Able
Ace
Achill
Adam
Adonis
Ajax
Aladdin
Aldo
Alex
Alf
Ali
Alk
Allah
Amor
Appolo
Arco
Argo
Ariel
Armin
Arno
Arrak
Arras
Artemis
Artus
Asco
Assi
Astor
Atlas
Atos
Attila
Atzel
Axel

Baldur
Barko
Baron
Bass
Beau
Bello
Bengel
Benje
Benno
Bento
Berndt
Bill
Bimbo
Bingo
Bismark
Blick
Blitz
Bodo
Bonze
Boris
Bosko
Brisco
Brix
Bruno
Brutus
Buck

Caesar
Captain
Carlo
Castor
Cato
Cent

Chris
Cid
Cirro
Cisko
Cito
Claus
Colt
Comet
Conde
Condor
Conrad
Costa
Count
Cuno
Curt
Cyrus

Dago
Dallo
Damon
Dandy
Dan (ny)
Dargo
Dax
Dido
Dietz
Dingo
Dino
Dirk
Doktor
Dolf

Don (ny)
Donar
Dorn
Drago
Droll
Duck (y)
Duke
Dunder
Duro
Duse
Dux

Ebing
Ebony
Echos
Edel
Egon
Egor
Eko
Elch
Elf
Elk
Emir
Enno
Erf
Erich
Erko
Ernst
Eros
Esser
Esso
Etzel
Evan
Ezra

Falk
Faust
Fedor
Felix
Fello
Fels
Ferdi
Flag
Flash
Flint
Flott
Franco
Franz
Freddy
Frei
Frig
Fritz
Fürst

Geno
Gernot
Gero
Gert
Giles
Goetz
Golo
Graf
Grandee
Greif
Gunar
Gustel

Hal (lo)
Hanko
Hans

Hansel
Harros
Hassan
Hasso
Hawk
Heido (i)
Heinrigh
Heinz & Kunz
  (Tom, Dick
  and Harry)
Hektor
Hercule (s)
Hero
Herr
Hessian
Hort
Hugo
Hummel
Hussan

Ibo
Igor
Ilk
Immo
Ingo
Ira
Isar
Isko
Itmus

Jäger
Jago
Jake
Jankus

Jasper
Joe (y)
Johann
Jon
Jorg
Jucker
Junker
Juno
Junos

Kaiser
Kalif
Karlo
Kasper
Kay
Keck
Klaus
Kobold
Komet
Konig
Konrad
Kraft
Kreig
Kuno
Kurt
Kyras

Lalla
Lancer
Landor
Larry
Leon
Lex
Lipp
Lord

Lucky
Ludwig
Luke
Lümmel
Lutz
Lux
Lynz

Major
Mark (o)
Markus
Mars
Meister
Mentor
Michel
Milo
Mingo
Mirko
Moritz
Morris
Murr

Necker
Ned (dy)
Nemo
Nero
Nestor
Nick
Nickolas
Nimrod
Nock
Nomad
Norman
Nox

Odin
Omar
Onkus
Orkus
Orno
Orphus
Oskar
Ossi
Otis
Otto
Owen

Pandur
Panther
Pascha
Pasco
Pat (rick)
Peter
Petz
Pfeffer
Pleck
Pol
Pollux
Prince

Quail
Quandu (s)
Quell
Quick
Quinn
Quint
Quinton
Quitt
Quixote

Ranger
Rappo
Rauck
Remo
Rex
Richter
Ringo
Rino
Robb
Rodger
Rogue
Rolf
Rollo
Rommel
Rudy
Rusty

Saber
Sager
Sago
Sam (son)
Sarto
Satan
Saxon
Schanz
Sepp (el)
Severn
Sieg
Siegfred
Simon
Solo (man)
Speck
Stolz
Sylvanus

Tasso
Teddy
Tell
Tellus
Terry
Theo
Toby
Tony
Treff
Treu
Trojan
Troy
Trudel
Tyrus

Udo
Ulk
Ulrich
Ulysses
Unkus
Uno
Uri
Urian
Ursus
Utz

Val
Valko
Veit
Vidal
Viktor
Vincenz
Vitus
Vock

Volk
Von

Wagner
Waldin
Waldo
Wally
Wehrwolf
Widu
Wilfred
Wilhelm
Wodan

Xandu
Xavier
Xell
Xerres
Xerxes
Xot

Yogi
York
Yuno
Yurri

Zampa
Zar
Zarek
Zeb
Zett
Zeus
Zitt
Zobel
Zoltan
Zorn

Right, German Shorthaired Pointer. Axel v. Madersbach (Germany).

Left, German Wirehaired Pointer. Ch. Mueller Mill's Valentino, owned by Helen Case Shelly, Roanoke, Texas.

Popular Affixes for German Names

Au(e)—Green pasture, meadow
Alm—Alpine Meadow
Bach—Brook
Berg—Mountain, hill
Brunnen—Well, fountain
Brücke—Bridge
Burg—Castle, fortress
Dorf—Village
Edel—Noble, aristocratic
Ehre—Honor, distinction
Erde—Earth, ground, soil
Feld—Field
Flinte—Gun
Freund—Friend
Friede—Peace
Forst—Forest
Gross—Great, large
Grund—Ground
Hauch—Breath
Haus—House
Heide—Heathen
Heim—Home
Herz—Heart, courage
Hock—High
Hof—Courtyard, farm, inn, lodge
Höhe—Height
Hold—Kind, friendly, gracious
Holz—Wood, timber
Honig—Honey
Hügel—Hill
Hund—Dog
Hundehütte—Kennel
Hundin—Female dog, bitch
Jagd—Hunt
Jäger—Hunter
Kraft—Strength, vigor

Left, Weimaraner. Ch. Mokelumne's Silver Kachina, owned by J. and E. Hickman, Modesto, California.

Below, Giant Schnauzer. Ch. H-Starrs Aquarius, owned by Jim and Starr Henderson, Baldwin Park, California.

Kreuz—Cross
Kühle—Cool, fresh
Lieb—Dear, beloved, good
Liebe—Love
Liebchen—Sweetheart
Licht—Light
Mark—Coin, boundary
Marke—Brand, trademark
Meister—Master, champion
Muhle—Mill, grinder, game
Preis—Prize
Rand—Edge, border
Reich—Kingdom, empire
Reich—Rich, wealthy
Rein—Clean pure
Ruhm—Glory, fame
Schatz—Treasure
Schau—Show
Scheideweg—Crossroads
Scheu—Shy, skittish
Schloss—Castle, palace, lock
Schön—Beautiful
Staat—State
Stadt—Town, city
Strasse—Road
Sieger—Champion Dog, Victor
Siegerin—Champion Bitch
Stammbaum—Pedigree, family tree
Strand—Beach, shore
Strom—Stream
Sturm—Storm
Tal—Valley, dale, glen
Tor—Gate, door
Wache—Guard, sentry
Wald—Road, a way, course
Wasser—Water
Weg—Road, a way, course
Weide—Pasture, willow
Welt—World

FAMILY RELATIONSHIPS

Ancestor—Ahn
Aunt—Tante
Boy—Knabe
Brother—Bruder
Brother-in-Law—Schwager
Child—Kind
Cousin (male)—Vetter, Cousin
Cousin (female)—Base, Kusine
Daughter—Tochter
Daughter-in-Law—Schwiegertochter
Descendant—Nachkomme
Family—Familie
Father—Vater
Father-in-law—Schwiegervater
Forefather—Ahne, Vorvater
Friend (male)—Freund
Friend (female)—Freundin
Gentleman, Sir, Mr.—Herr
Girl—Mädchen
Grandchild (male)—Enkel
Grandchild (female)—Enkelin
Grandfather—Grossvater
Grandmother—Grossmutter
Grandparents—Grosseltern
Grand Uncle—Grossonkle
Granny—Oma
Great Granddaughter—Urenkelin
Great Grandfather—Urgrossvater
Great Grandmother—Urgrossmutter
Great Grandson—Urenkel
Husband—Gatte
Kin, family—Verwandtschaft
Kinship—Sippe
Mother—Mutter
Mother-in-Law—Schwiegermutter
Parents—Eltern
Sister—Schwester
Sister-in-Law—Schwägerin

Son—Sohn
Son-in-Law—Schwiegersohn
Stepbrother—Stiefbruder
Stepchild—Stiefkind
Stepdaughter—Stieftochter
Stepfather—Stiefeltern
Stepmother—Stiefmutter
Stepparents—Stiefeltern
Stepson—Stiefsohn
Uncle—Onkel
Woman, Wife—Frau
Young Lady, Miss—Fräulein
Youth—Jugend
Youthful—Jugendlich

CARDINAL NUMBERS

One—eins
Two—zwei
Three—drei
Four—vier
Five—fünf
Six—sechs
Seven—sieben
Eight—acht
Nine—neun
Ten—zehn

ORDINAL NUMBERS

First—erste
Second—zweite
Third—dritte
Fourth—vierte
Fifth—fünfte
Sixth—sechste
Seventh—siebte
Eighth—achte
Ninth—neunte
Tenth—zehnte

THE FOUR SEASONS

Spring—Frühling
Summer—Sommer
Autumn—Herbst
Winter—Winter

THE MONTHS

January—Januar
February—Februar
March—März
April—April
May—Mai
June—Juni
July—Juli
August—August
September—September
October—Oktober
November—November
December—Dezember

THE DAYS OF THE WEEK

Sunday—Sonntag
Monday—Montag
Tuesday—Dienstag
Wednesday—Mittwoch
Thursday—Donnerstag
Friday—Freitag
Saturday—Samstag (South Germany and Austria)
　　　　　—Sonnabend (North Germany)

WORDS RELATING TO TIME

Minute—Minute
Hour—Stunde
Day—Tag
Week—Woche
Month—Monat
Year—Jahr
Century—Jahrhundert
Today—Heute
Tomorrow—Übermorgen, *the day after.*
Morning—Morgen
Yesterday—Gestern
Dawn—Morgengrauen
Forenoon—Vormittag
Afternoon—Nachmittag
Evening—Abend
Dusk—Dämmerung
Night—Nacht
Time—Zeit
Early—Frühe
Late—Spät
East-ern—Ost, östlich
West-ern—Westen, westlich
Central—Zentral
North-ern—Norden, nordlich
South-ern—Süden, südlich
Sun—Sonne
Moon—Mond
Star—Stern
Sky—Himmel

TREES, SHRUBS, AND RELATED TERMS

Acacia—Akazie
Acre—Acker
Almond—Mandel
Apple—Apfel
Apricot—Aprikose
Ash—Esche
Aspen—Espe
Balsam—Balsam
Bamboo—Bambus
Beech tree—Buche
Birch—Birke
Bush—Busch
Camphor—Kampfer
Cedar—Zeder
Cherry—Kirschbaum
Cypress—Zypress
Ebony—Ebenholz
Elm—Ulme
Evergreen—Immergrün
Fig tree—Feige
Fir—Tanne, Fichte
Forest—Wald
Grape—Weintraube
Grove—Hain
Heather—Heidekraut
Juniper—Wacholder
Laurel—Lorbeer
Leaf—Blatt
Lemon—Zitrone
Lilac—Flieder, Elder
Lime—Linde, Linden
Mahogany—Mahagoni
Maple—Ahorn
Mulberry—Maulbeere
Oak—Eiche
Olive—Olive
Orange—Orange
Orchard—Obstgarten
Palm—Palme

Peach Tree—Pfirsich
Pear Tree—Birne
Pine—Fichte, Kiefer
Plum Tree—Pflaume
Pomegranate—Granatapfel
Poplar—Pappel
Rosemary—Rosmarin
Rosewood—Rosenholz
Sapling—Bäumchen
Spruce—Fichte
Tree—Baum
Vine—Weinstock
Walnut—Walnuss
Willow—Weide
Wood—Holz
Yew—Eibe

JEWELS

Agate—Achat
Amethyst—Amethyst
Coral—Koralle
Diamond—Diamant
Emerald—Smaragd
Gem—Gemme
Garnet—Granat
Jade—Jade
Jewel—Juwel
Onyx—Onyx
Opal—Opal
Pearl—Pearle
Precious Jewel—Edelstein
Ruby—Rubin
Sapphire—Saphir
Stone—Stein
Topaz—Topas
Turquoise—Turkis

FLOWERS AND RELATED TERMS

Anemone—Anemone, Windröschen
Aster—Aster
Azalea—Azalie
Bloom—Blume
Blossom—Blüte
Bluebell—Glochenblume
Bouquet—Bukett
Camellia—Camelli
Carnation, pink—Nelke
Chrysanthemum—Chrysantheme
Daffodil, yellow—Gelbe Narzisse
Dahlia—Dahlie
Daisy—Gänseblümchen
Dandelion—Löwenzahn
Fern—Farn
Flower—Blume
Garden—Garten
Gardenia—Gardenie
Honeysuckle—Geissblatt
Hyacinth—Hyazinthe
Iris—Schwertlilie
Ivy—Efeu
Jasmine—Jasmin
Lily—Lilie—*of the Valley*
　　　　　—das Maiglöchchen
Marigold—Dotterblume
Morning Glory—Morgenblühen
Nasturtium—Gartenkresse
Orchid—Orchidee
Pansy—Stiefmütterchen
Poppy—Mohn
Primrose—Primel
Rose—Rose
Tulip—Tulpe
Violet—Veilchen
Water Lily—Wasserlilie

THE COLORS

Amber—Bernstein
Apricot—Apricose
Azure blue—Himmelblau, Azurblau
Black—Schwarz
Blue—Blau
Bronze—Bronze
Brown—Braun
Buff—Lederfarben, *leather color*
Carmine Red—Karminrot
Color—Farbe
Coral—Koralle
Crimson—Karmesin
Ebony—Ebenholz
Golden—Golden
Gray—Grau
Green—Grün
Hyacinth—Hyazinthe
Ivory—Elfenbein
Jade—Jade
Lavender—Lavendel
Lilac (color)—Lila
Maroon—Kastanlenbraun
Mulberry—Maulbeere
Olive—Olive
Orange—Orange
Orchid—Orchidee
Pink—Rosa
Purple—Purpurn
Red—Rot
Rose—Rose
Ruby—Rubin
Rust—Rost
Sapphire—Saphir
Silver—Silber
Violet—Veilchen
White—Weiss
Yellow—Gelb

Specialized Listings

COAT COLORS IN GERMAN DOGS

Abzeichen—Markings

Blau—Blue

Blesse—Blaze, mark on head or muzzle

Braun—Brown, plain, solid

Braun—Brown with minor white or speckled markings on chest and legs

Braunschimmel*—Brown and gray (white) with brown head, brown patches and/or dots

Brustfleck—White or speckled markings on chest

Bunt Farbe—Bright, gay, motley, variegated, spotted

Drathaar—Wirehair

Dreifarbig—Three colored, tri-colored

Dunkel—Dark

Dunkelbraun—Dark Brown

Dunkelbraunschimmel—Dark brown and gray (white) with brown head, brown patches and/or dots

Dunkelrot—Dark Red

Eichfarbig—Elk colored (brown mixture)

Einfarbig—Self-colored, one color, plain

Farbe—Color

Fleckig—Spotted, speckled

Forellen—Pure, entire solid of color

Gelb—Yellow, amber

Gestreift—Brindle, striped

Gestrommt—Brindle

Glanz—Lustrous, glossy

Glatthaarig—Smooth coated

Grau—Grey

Grau, meliert—Gray, grizzled

Haar—Hair, coat

Haarlos—Hairless

Hell—Bright or light color

Hellbraunschimmel—Light brown and gray (white) with brown head, brown patches and/or dots

Hellschimmel—Light gray/white mixture

Hirschrot—Reddish Fawn

* In some Standards, the colors *Braunschimmel* and *Dunkelbraunschimmel* have a base color that is not brown and white, or white with brown, but the hair shows a complete mixture of BROWN and GRAY (white) such as in German Shorthaird Pointers. The color of the head is mostly brown, often with speckled areas on top of the muzzle and on top of the skull and with speckled flews. In some Standards, black color is permitted in the same combinations as brown. (Deutsch-Kurzhaar-Verbandes.)

52

Kurzhaar (-ig)—Shorthair, Shorthaired
Langhaar (-ig)—Longhair, longhaired
Meltau—Mildew, brand, stigma
Pfeger und Salz—Pepper and Salt
Plattern—Patches
Rot—Red
Rötlich—Reddish
Rothaarig—Redhaired
Rotschimmel—Roan
Rost—Rust
Saddle—Sattel
Scheck—Piebald or dappled animal (See Bunt)
Scheckig—Parti-colored, spotted, mottled, brindled
Schimmel—Gray or white horse; become gray
Schimmeln—Become gray, turn gray
Schwarz—Black
Schwarzgelb—Tawny, dark yellow
Schwarzgrau—Black-gray mixture
Schwarzschimmel—Iron gray
Schwarz mit Braunen Abzeichen—Black with brown markings (Black and Tan)
Schwarz mit Rostbraun—Black with rust-brown
Schwarzgrau mit Abzeichen—Black with gray markings
Silbergrau—Silver gray
Sprenkel—Speckle
Sprenkelig—Speckled
Tiefschwarz—Solid black
Tupfen, Fleck—Dot, Spot
Weiss—White
Zottig—Shaggy
Zwillich—Ticking

Example of the *Schwarzschimmel* coat color—Quell Pöttmes (V), German Shorthaired Pointer.

BIRDS

Bird—Vogel
Blackbird—Amsel
Canary—Kanarien
Chicken—Huhn Hünchen
Cockatoo—Kakadu
Duck—Ente
Eagle—Adler
Falcon—Falke
Finch—Fink
Flamingo—Flamingo
Flock—Schwarm
Game—Wild
Goose—Gans
Gosling—Gänschen
Hawk—Habicht
Hen—Henne
Hummingbird—Kolibri
Lark, Skylark—Lerche
Meadow—Wiese
Meadowlark—Feldlerche
Nightingale—Nachtigall
Owl—Eule
Parrot—Papagei
Partridge—Rebhuhn
Peacock—Pfau
Pheasant—Fasan
Pigeon—Taube
Quail—Wachtel
Robin—Rotkehlchen
Rooster—Hahn
Sparrow—Sperling, Spatz
Swallow—Schwalbe
Swan—Schwan
Thrush—Drossle
Woodlark—Heidelerche
Woodpecker—Specht
Wren—Zäunkonig

POPULAR NAMES OF DISTINCTION

Actor—Schauspieler
Actress—Schauspielerin
Admiral—Admiral
Baron—Baron, Freiherr
Baroness—Baronin, Freiherrin
Baronial—Freiherrlich
Bishop—Bishof
Captain—Kapitän
Cavalier—Reiter, Kavalier
Chief—Oberhaupt (head, chief, sovereign)
Colonel—Colonel, Oberst
Commander—Komandant
Corporal—Korporal
Count—Gräf
Countess—Gräfinnen
Diplomat—Diplomat
Director—Direktor
Doctor—Doktor
Duke—Herzöge
Duchess—Herzögenen
Emperor—Kaiser
Empress—Kaiserin
General—General, Feldherr
Judge—Richter
King—König
Lady—Lady, Dame
Leader—Fuhrer
Lord—Herr
Major—Major
Master, Champion—Meister
Monarch—Monarch
Pal—Kamerad
Prince—Fürst
Princess—Fürsten
Queen—Königin

Marienburg, the castle of the Master of the Teutonic Knights.

CASTLES

Germany's countryside is sprinkled with castles and cathedrals—with secular and ecclesiastical architecture—hallmarks of this country's interesting land. In addition there are the imperial palaces, mansions, monasteries, and abbeys. At strategic locations are fortresses, many dating back to the Middle Ages, their walled towers reaching skyward where the magnificent view of the world below is more spectacular than the cliffs they dominate.

There are *Wasserburgen* (Water Castles) built close to the banks of lowland rivers or by the shores of lakes in the hill areas and Alpine resorts. The banks and heights of the Rhine, Germany's most navigable and important river, are dotted with differing types of castles—widely influenced in structure and varying from Romanesque to Gothic.

The Germans were celebrated hunters in antiquity, and hunting has remained one of the lasting passions close to their hearts. Thus, it is not at all remarkable that there are as many famous Jagdschloss (hunting castles) as palatial and baronial mansions. Because of Germany's location in Europe, the Germans, through the centuries, were often resisting invasion, or were at war or under siege, which must have left little time for sports. Yet most hunting courts and wealthy land owners were involved in the early culture of raising dogs, whether it concerned protection against predators, hunting, coursing, or selective breeding.

The *Sondershausen Castle* (now in East Germany) was a great hunting court about the year 1714. It was said to possess only "three Pointers" which were in constant use to obtain the allotted game quota, but several young ones were withheld for breeding. A century later, Pointers were said to be still "as much in demand as they were scarce." Another famous hunting lodge was *Heidelberg Castle* on the Necker River, now in partial ruins except for the forepart of the castle which has been preserved. The great frescoed dome, the mosaics, wall tapestries, and other accouterments may be seen today via tours.

Many of the old knights' fortresses have roots that evolved from the earliest centuries. The *Burg Hirschhorn*, near Heidelberg, was a powerful stronghold that was built about the twelfth century. The name means deer-stag horn. It housed the Knights of Hirschhorn for nearly four centuries, and with its deep moat it became a refuge for people living outside the great walls.

The *Water Castle Anholt* in Westphalia, near the Holland border, is interesting, for this is where the *Princes zu Solms* lived, owners since about the sixteenth century. Lying in the corridor of constant invasions, this castle was damaged severely but renewed at great expense after the last war. About 1875, *Prince Albrecht zu Solms-Bronfels* was devoted and successful in guiding the development of various types of hunting dogs—and in judging them as well. His work was acknowledged when German Shorthair fanciers renamed their Annual Fall Breed Search "Prince Solms Memorial Search" in his honor. Also, German immigrants to the United States commemorated his name by naming a town in Texas "New Bronfels."

It is not possible to cover here the lengthy history of castles in Germany, but they are everywhere—from the north along the Rhine River, south to the Rhineland-Palatinate, to the areas of Wurttemberg and Bavaria, as well as along the Isar River where trade routes crossed in the Middle Ages. There are the famous castles of the Danube River, which flows through the area between Munich and Nuremberg. Included here is *Neuschwanstein Castle*, said to have been one of King Ludwig's finest.

Many names appropriate for kennels will be found on the castle map of Germany, reproduced on the end sheets of this book, which is interesting for its concise information. Published in the book *Castle Hotels of Europe*, copyrighted by Robert P. Long, the map is reproduced here through special permission from Mr. Long.

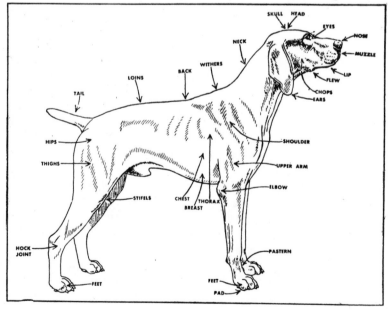

GERMAN NAMES FOR ANALYTICAL PARTS OF A DOG'S BODY

Angulated—Winkelung
Arm, Forearm—Arm, Vorderarm
Back—Rücke
Bone—Knochen, Bein
Brisket, Breast—Brust
Cheek—Backe
Collar—Halsband, Kragen
Croup, Rump—Kruppe
Ear (s)—Ohr (en)
Elbow, Forearm—Ellbogen
Eye (s)—Auge (n)
Flews—Lefzen (of hounds)
Forechest—Vorderbrust
Forepaw—Vorderpfote
Forequarters—Vorderhand
Head—Kopf
Hindlegs—Hinterläüfe
Hindquarters—Hinterteil
Hip, Haunch—Huft-e
Hock, Ankle Joint—Sprunggelenk
Leg—Bein
Lip—Lippe
Loin—Lende
Long—Lang
Muzzle, Snout—Schnauz-e
Neck—Hals
Nose—Nase
Paw, Foot—Pfote, Pfoten
Ribs—Rippe
Short—Kurz
Shoulder—Schulter
Skull—Schädel
Stifle, Knee—Kniegelenk
Stop—Punkt
Tail—Rute, Schwanz
Thigh—Oberschenkel
Thorax—Brust
Withers—Widderist

GERMAN VOCABULARY RELATING TO DOGS

Abstammung—Origin, descent, ancestry
Abzeichen—Markings
Achtung—Look out! Careful! On guard!
Ahnentafel—Family tree, pedigree
Alt(er)—Old, (aged)
Angekört—Inspected, certified suitable for breeding
Ankörung—Official inspection for breeding suitability
Apportierbock—Dumbbell (used in training)
Apporttieren (of dogs)—Fetch, retrieve
Aus—Out! out of, from
Ausbildung—Improvement of a breed
Ausstellung—Display, show exhibition
Band, Bände—Volume, volumes (magazine or book)
Befehl—Command (order used in training)
Befriedigend—Satisfactory (rating used in show points)
Begleithunde—Companion, escort, house dogs
Belassen—Leave alone, stay with dam after birth
Belegt—Bred, of bitches
Besitzer(in)—Owner, male (female)
Bewertung—Valuation rating (excellent, very good, poor)
Bild, Bilder—Picture, pictures
Bleibsitzen—Stay
Blindenfuhrer Hund—Guide dog for the blind
Bring(en)—Fetch, (to fetch)
Brustgeschirr—Dog harness
Daun—Down! Halt! (in training)
Decken—To breed, cover by a stud
Decktag—Breeding date
Diensthund—Service dog (trained in service)
Dienstsuchhund—Tracking dog in police duty
Dienstsuchhundprüfung—Tracking dog trial or contest
Dressierung—Training
Dritter—Third
Ehrenpreis—Trophy
Eingetragener Verein—Registered Association or Club
Eintragung—Entry in show or registered in stud book
Erster—First
Federation Cynologique Internationale—International Dog Federation which awards World Championship Titles

Fehler—Faults
Führer—Leader, handler
Fuss—Heel!
Gebrauchshund—Utility working dog
Gedeckt—Bred, covered
Genügend—Satisfactory, sufficient
Geschutzter Zuchtname—Registered kennel name
Gewörfen—Whelped
Gross—Big, large
Grösse—Size
Gut—Good
Hauptprüfung—Championship contest or trial
Hervorragend—Distinguished
Hitze—Heat, season in bitches
Höhe—Height
Hund, Hunde—Dog, dogs
Hundefraunde—Dog lovers, fanciers
Hündin, Hündinnen—Bitch, bitches
Inzucht—Inbreeding
Jung(en)—Young, to bring forth young
Jungtier—Young animal, puppy
Katalog—Catalog
Klein—Little, small, tiny
Kleine—Little one, little child, sweetheart
Kleintierzüchter—Small animal breeder
Klubsieger—Club Champion Dog
Klubsiegerin—Club Champion Bitch
Körzeichen—Certified suitable for breeding
Kräftig—Strong
Kriegshund—War dog
Laüfe—Running action, legs
Legen—Lie Down!
Leine—Leash
Leistung—Field training, achievement testing
Leistungprüfung—Field Trial
Leistungssieger (in)—Field Trial Champion, male (female)
Liebhaber—Fancier
Mangelhaft—Faulty, lacking
Maske—Mask, face
Meldeschein—Registration Certificate
Meldung—Entry, registration

Nummer—Number
O—Zero, failed
Offenklasse—Open Class
Paar—Pair, brace
Pfeger und Salz—Pepper and Salt
Plaz—Place (in competition)
Polizehund—Police-trained dog (any breed)
Preis, Preise—Prize, prizes
Preishüten—Herding Trial
Preishüten Sieger (in)—Herding Champion, dog (bitch)
Prüfung—Performance test or trial
Rasse—Race, breed
Rassehund—Pedigreed dog
Rein—Pure, entire, solid (color)
Reinzucht—Purebred
Richter—Judge
Rüde—Large Hound, male animal
Sanitätshund—First Aid Dog (Red Cross)
Sattel—Saddle
Schäferhund—Shepherd Dog
Schau—Show
Schönheit—Beauty
Schönheitsieger—Bench Champion
Sehr gut—Very good
Setzen—Sit!
Sieger (in)—Champion, dog (bitch)
Siegerausstellung—Championship Show
Sonderausstellung—Specialty Show
Sonderverein—Specialty Club
Such—Search, follow a trail
Suchhund der Polizei—Police tracker
Suchhundprüfung—Trailing Test
Teckel—Dachshund
Tier—Animal
Ubekannt—Unknown
Ubung—Training exercise
Ungenugend—Unsatisfactory
Verbindung—Mating
Verein—Club or Association
Vierter—Fourth

Vorpüfung—Preliminary trial
Vorsitzender—President, Chairman
Vorzuglich (V)—Excellent (highest rating)
Wanderpreis—Challenge Trophy (Best of Breed)
Wasserhundprüfung—Water Dog Trial
Weiss—White
Weitsprung—Broad jump
Welp (en)—Young puppy (puppies)
Weltsieger (in)—World Champion, dog (bitch)
Werfen—To produce, to whelp
Wurf—Litter
Wurfdatum—Whelping date
Wurfstärke—Litter size, number
Zucht—Breeding, breed, race, rearing
Zuchtbuch—Studbook
Züchter (in)—Breeder, male (female)
Zuchthündin—Brood bitch.
Zuchtpreis—Bred by exhibitor prize
Zuchtverein—Specialty Club
Zulassung—Allowed, permitted
Zweiter—Second
Zwingburg—Stronghold
Zwinger—Kennel
Zwingername—Kennel name
Zwillich (e)—Tick (ing)
Zwilling—Twins

WÄCHTER DER REICHEN
FREUND DES ARMEN,
DAS EINZIGE GESCHÖPP
DAS TREU IST BIS ZUM TODE.*

*The rich man's guardian and the poor man's friend, the only creature faithful to the end.

GERMANY

KIEL
Voss-Haus
Tremsbüttel
HAMBURG
Gehrhus
BERLIN
HOLLAND
Petershagen
E3
HANOVER
E8
E. GERMANY
E8
Wilkinghege
Anholt
MÜNSTER Hohenfeld
Arensburg
Lembeck
Schwalenberg
Achtermann
Engelsburg
E3
Berge
ESSEN DORTMUND
Trendelburg
Sababurg
DÜSSELDORF
Hugenpoet
Gastätte
Rheydt
Hohenscheid
Schnellenberg
KASSEL
Berlepsch
Wassenberg
Georghausen
Waldeck
Spangenberg
COLOGNE
Auel
BONN Wasserburg
Godesburg (Hennef-Sieg)
Ockenfels
Staufenberg
Burghaus
Alte
Klostermühle
KOBLENZ
E5
Holzberg
Lauenstein
Alte Thorschenke
Ehrenburg
Cleeberg
Ronneburg
Neustadt
HOF
Rheinfels
Waffenschmiede
Sonnenhof
Gattendorf
Malberg
Schönburg
Kronberg
Saaleck
Bettenburg
Banz
Reichenstein
WIESBADEN
FRANKFURT
Krone
MAINZ
Dürnhof
Thiergarten
Niederwald
Kranichstein
Steinburg
WÜRZBURG
Rabenstein
TRIER
E6
MOSEL
Fuchs'sche Mühle
Hirschhorn
Weikersheim
MANNHEIM
Neuburg
Goldener Hirsch
NÜRNBERG
Kropsburg
HEIDELBERG
Guttenberg
Gottenburg
Stetten
Gebsattel
Hornberg
Heinsheim
Lehen
Friedrichsruhe
Abenberg
HEILBRONN
Eggersberg
Englburg
Vellberg
Deutsches Haus
Falkenfels
Aicha
Bauschlott
Ort
FRANCE
Badischer
Windeck
STUTTGART
Solitude
Sindlingen
Weitenburg
AUGSBURG
MUNICH
Grunwald
Königsegg
RAVENSBURG
Seeon
Wasserburg
(Bodensee)
Marquartstein
SWITZERLAND
AUSTRIA

Published in the book *Castle Hotels of Europe*, copyrighted by
Robert P. Long, this map is reproduced here through special
permission from Mr. Long.